I want to be a Librarian

I WANT TO BE A

Librarian

DAN LIEBMAN

FIREFLY BOOKS

A FIREFLY BOOK

Published by Firefly Books Ltd. 2003

Copyright © 2003 Firefly Books Ltd.

First Printing 2003

**Publisher Cataloging-in-Publication Data (U.S.)
(Library of Congress Standards)**

Liebman, Dan.
   I want to be a librarian / Dan Liebman.—1st ed.
[24] p. : col. photos. ; cm.   –(I want to be)
Summary: Photographs and easy-to-read text describe the job of a librarian.
ISBN 1-55297-691-2
ISBN 1-55297-689-0 (pbk.)
1. Librarians – Vocational guidance 2. Occupations. I. Title. II. Series
331.124102 21   HD8039.L53.L54   2003

Published in the United States in 2003 by
Firefly Books (U.S.) Inc.
P.O. Box 1338, Ellicott Station
Buffalo, New York, USA, 14205

**National Library of Canada Cataloguing in
Publication Data**

Liebman, Daniel
   I want to be a Librarian

ISBN 1-55297-691-2 (bound)
ISBN 1-55297-689-0 (pbk.)

1. Librarians– Juvenile literature. I. Title.

Z682.L54 2003   j020'.23   C2002-903691-7

Published in Canada in 2003 by
Firefly Books Ltd.
3680 Victoria Park Avenue
Toronto, Ontario, Canada, M2H 3K1

Photo Credits

© AP Photo/Jacqueline Roggenbrodt, pages 10-11

© Harry Cutting Photography, page 9

© Chip Henderson/MaXx Images, front cover, page 18

© Mark E. Gibson Stock Photography, pages 6-7

© Monroe County Public Library; Bloomington, IN, page 23

© SW Productions/Getty Images, page 12

© George Walker/Firefly Books, pages 5, 8, 13, 14, 15, 16, 17,
   19, 20-21, 22, 24, back cover

The author and publisher would like to thank:

Baycrest Centre for Geriatric Care, Toronto
Inta McCaughey, Bruce Public School, Toronto
Katherine Quan, Jones Public Library, Toronto
Saira Mall, Greg Patterson and
V.W. Bladen Library at University of Toronto at Scarborough
Debbie Johnson-Houston

Design by Interrobang Graphic Design Inc.
Printed and bound in Canada by Friesens, Altona, Manitoba

The Publisher acknowledges the financial support of the Government of Canada through the Book Publishing Industry Development Program for its publishing activities.

Librarians help people find the books they want.

This student is working on a project. The librarian has helped her find the right book.

Librarians choose the books for the library. These children like all the new books.

With a library card, you can borrow books.

Librarians help explain things to people.

The computer catalog helps people find what they're looking for.

Librarians or their helpers put materials back on the shelves. A helper is called a "page."

This girl likes animal stories. The librarian shows her an interesting book.

This librarian works in a hospital. She helps doctors and nurses find information.

This children's librarian is reading out loud. Every week there is a special storybook afternoon.

There are libraries in schools and colleges.

Sometimes, the library goes to the readers. A traveling library is called a "bookmobile."

Librarians have a busy job. But who could be better than sharing a book with other people?